T0322251

Master Maths at Home

Algebra and Extra Challenges

Scan the QR code to help your child's learning at home.

DK | MATHS NO PROBLEM!

How to use this book

Maths — No Problem! created **Master Maths at Home** to help children develop fluency in the subject and a rich understanding of core concepts.

Key features of the Master Maths at Home books include:

- Carefully designed lessons that provide structure, but also allow flexibility in how they're used.

- Speech bubbles containing content designed to spark diverse conversations, with many discussion points that don't have obvious 'right' or 'wrong' answers.

- Rich illustrations that will guide children to a discussion of shapes and units of measurement, allowing them to make connections to the wider world around them.

- Exercises that allow a flexible approach and can be adapted to suit any child's cognitive or functional ability.

- Clearly laid-out pages that encourage children to practise a range of higher-order skills.

- A community of friendly and relatable characters who introduce each lesson and come along as your child progresses through the series.

You can see more guidance on how to use these books at **mastermathsathome.com**.

We're excited to share all the ways you can learn maths!

Copyright © 2022 Maths — No Problem!

Maths — No Problem!
mastermathsathome.com
www.mathsnoproblem.com
hello@mathsnoproblem.com

First published in Great Britain in 2022 by
Dorling Kindersley Limited
One Embassy Gardens, 8 Viaduct Gardens, London SW11 7BW
A Penguin Random House Company

The authorised representative in the EEA is Dorling Kindersley
Verlag GmbH. Arnulfstr. 124, 80636 Munich, Germany

10 9 8 7 6 5 4 3 2 1
001–327110–May/22

A CIP catalogue record for this book is available from the British Library.

ISBN: 978-0-24153-954-5
Printed and bound in the UK

For the curious
www.dk.com

This book was made with Forest Stewardship Council™ certified paper – one small step in DK's commitment to a sustainable future. For more information go to www.dk.com/our-green-pledge

Acknowledgements
The publisher would like to thank the authors and consultants Andy Psarianos, Judy Hornigold, Adam Gifford and Dr Anne Hermanson.

The Castledown typeface has been used with permission from the Colophon Foundry.

Contents

Ruby   Elliott   Amira   Charles   Lulu   Sam   Oak   Holly   Ravi   Emma   Jacob   Hannah

Describing patterns

Starter

Charles made a pattern using triangles.
How can we describe the rule of the pattern?

Example

Pattern number	Number of rows	Number of triangles in the bottom row
1	1	1
2	2	2
3	3	3
4	4	4
5	5	5
n	n	n

We can use a letter (n) to stand for any number.

So if $n = 100$ the pattern number 100 has 100 rows and 100 triangles in the bottom row.

Hannah made the following pattern.

  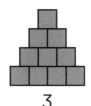 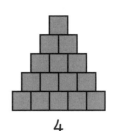

Pattern number:　　　1　　　　2　　　　3　　　　4

Pattern number	Number of rows	Number of squares in the bottom row
1	2	2
2	3	3
3	4	4
4	5	5
b	$b+1$	$b+1$

We can see that the number of rows is always one more than the pattern number.

We can also see that the number of squares in the bottom row is one more than the pattern number.

So if the pattern number is 100 or $b = 100$, then the figure will have 101 rows, $b + 1$, and there will be 101 squares in the bottom row, $b + 1$.

Practice

Use the following pattern to complete the table.

 1　　 2　　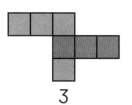 3　　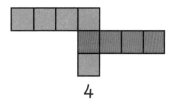 4

Pattern number	Number of pink squares	Number of green squares
1		
2		
3		
4		
5		
10		
a		

Algebraic expressions (part 1)

Starter

Ruby and Sam are playing a game.
When Sam says a number,
Ruby answers using a rule.
What is Ruby's rule?

Example

We say that Sam's number is the **input number**.

Ruby's number is the **output number**.

Input	1	2	3	4
Output	5	6	7	8

The output number is always 4 more than the input number.

We can use the algebraic expression, $a + 4$, to describe Ruby's rule.

The letter a can stand for any number.

Let's decide $a = 10$.
$a + 4 = 10 + 4$
$\qquad = 14$

When the input number, or a, is equal to 10, the output number is equal to 14.

We can give the input number different values.

$a = 50$

$a + 4 = 50 + 4$

$= 54$

$a = 100$

$a + 4 = 100 + 4$

$= 104$

$a = 500$

$a + 4 = 500 + 4$

$= 504$

Ravi joins the game and uses a different rule.

Input	2	4	6	8
Output	4	8	12	16

Each input number is multiplied by 2.

The algebraic expression is $2b$.

Practice

1 Use the algebraic expression $s + 5$ as the rule to complete the table.

Input	7	9	13	35	81
Output	12				

2 Use the algebraic expression $3c$ as the rule to complete the table.

Input	3	5	10	12	300
Output	9				

3 Write an algebraic expression to describe each rule. The first one has been done for you.

	input	output	input	output	input	output
(a)	2 → 7		10 → 15		m → $m + 5$	
(b)	4 → 12		6 → 18		w →	
(c)	9 → 18		12 → 21		s →	

Algebraic expressions (part 2)

Starter

Elliott and Oak completed their tables using different rules.

Input	4	5	9
Output	12	15	27

Input	6	12	18
Output	3	6	9

Elliott used the algebraic expression $3n$ to describe his rule.

Oak used the algebraic expression $\frac{x}{2}$ to describe her rule.

How can we use these algebraic expressions?

Example

$3n = 3 \times n$

The letter n is a variable. It can be any number.

When an algebraic expression is written this way we multiply n by 3.

So if $n = 4$, we can use this value as part of an equation.

$$3n = 3 \times n$$
$$= 3 \times 4$$
$$= 12$$

$$\frac{x}{2} = x \div 2$$

If $x = 6$, we can use this value as part of an equation.

$$\frac{x}{2} = x \div 2$$
$$= 6 \div 2$$
$$= 3$$

To **evaluate** an algebraic expression means to find the value of the expression.

Evaluate $3n$ when $n = 5$.

$3n = 3 \times n$
$\quad = 3 \times 5$
$\quad = 15$

Evaluate $\dfrac{x}{2}$ when $x = 12$.

$\dfrac{x}{2} = x \div 2$
$\quad = 12 \div 2$
$\quad = 6$

Practice

1 Write an algebraic expression in terms of **a**, to describe the rule that changes the input number to the output number.

input		output	input		output	input		output

(a) 10 → 5   16 → 8   a → ☐

(b) 5 → 20   7 → 28   a → ☐

2 Holly makes the following pattern using toothpicks.

  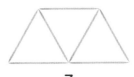 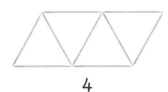

1   2   3   4

Evaluate $2n + 1$ when n has the following values. Complete the table.

Pattern number	Number of toothpicks
n	$2n + 1$
1	$2 \times 1 + 1 = 3$
2	$2 \times 2 + 1 = $ ☐
5	

Using simple formulae

Starter

A cafe offers all customers the chance to upgrade their main meal to a meal deal which includes a drink, a side dish and a dessert.

The cafe uses the formula $C = 1 + 2m$ to find the total cost of the meal deal.

What is the cost of Ravi's meal deal if he has fish and chips as his main meal?

Example

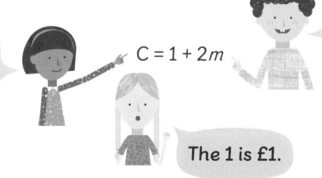

The letter C is the total cost of the meal deal.

$C = 1 + 2m$

The letter m is the price of the main meal. $2m = 2 \times m$

The 1 is £1.

The price of the fish and chips is £6. So $m = 6$.

$$C = 1 + 2m$$
$$= 1 + 2 \times 6$$
$$= 1 + 12$$
$$= 13$$

When $m = 6$, $C = 13$.

The cost of Ravi's meal deal is £13.

Find the cost of a meal deal with chicken curry as the main meal.

C = 1 + 2m

 m = 5.50

$\quad$ = 1 + 2 × 5.50

$\quad$ = 1 + 11

$\quad$ = 12

The cost of a meal deal with chicken curry as the main meal is £12.

Practice

1 The same cafe also has another deal. When customers buy 3 of the same main meal, the total cost is reduced by 40p.
The cafe uses the formula C = 3m – 0.40.

(a) Find the total cost of 3 cheese toasties.

m = 3.20

C = 3m – 0.40

$\quad$ = 3 × [ ] – 0.40

$\quad$ = [ ] – 0.40

$\quad$ = [ ]

The total cost of 3 cheese toasties is £ [ ].

(b) Find the total cost of 3 hot dogs.

m = [ ]

C = 3m – 0.40

The total cost of 3 hot dogs is £ [ ].

2 Use the formula $P = \dfrac{m}{4} + 2$ to find the value of P.

(a) m = 8

P = [ ]

(b) m = 11

P = [ ]

Equations and unknowns

Starter

What do we know about *a* and *b*?

$$a + b = 7$$

Example

a + *b* = 7 is an equation.

a	b	a + b = 7
1	6	1 + 6 = 7
2	5	2 + 5 = 7
3	4	3 + 4 = 7
4	3	4 + 3 = 7
5	2	5 + 2 = 7
6	1	6 + 1 = 7

The equals sign shows us that *a* + *b* must have a value equal to 7.

We can use different letters to stand for different numbers.

So if *a* = 1, then *b* = 6.

12

Jacob drew the following bar model.

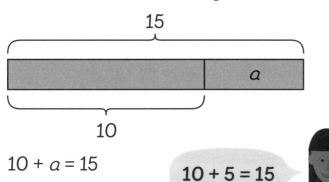

$10 + a = 15$
$a = 5$

$10 + 5 = 15$

We can use the equation $10 + a = 15$ to find the value of a.

Hannah drew the following bar model.

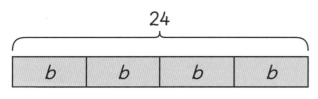

$4b = 24$
$b = 6$

$4 \times ? = 24$

Practice

1 What is the value of y in the following equations?

(a)

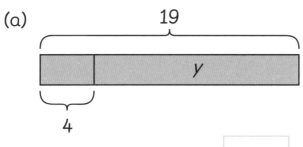

$4 + y = 19$ $\qquad y = \boxed{}$

(b)

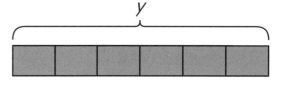

$\dfrac{y}{6} = 3$ $\qquad y = \boxed{}$

2 Find the value of s in the following equations.

(a) $13 + s = 27$ $\qquad s = \boxed{}$

(b) $45 - s = 36$ $\qquad s = \boxed{}$

(c) $5s = 60$ $\qquad s = \boxed{}$

(d) $2s + 10 = 26$ $\qquad s = \boxed{}$

(e) $40 - 5s = 15$ $\qquad s = \boxed{}$

Describing position using algebra

Starter

Vertices are shown on square A and square B.

I think I can describe the diagonally opposite vertex to (x, y) on square A as $(x + 3, y + 3)$.

Is Charles correct?
How can the vertex diagonally opposite (c, d) be described?

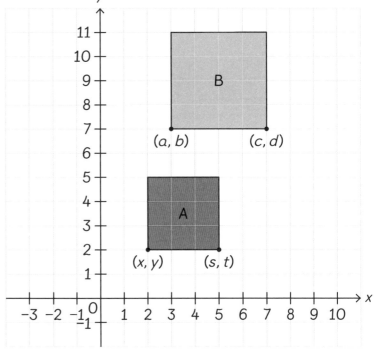

Example

Start by finding the coordinates of all the vertices on square A and square B.

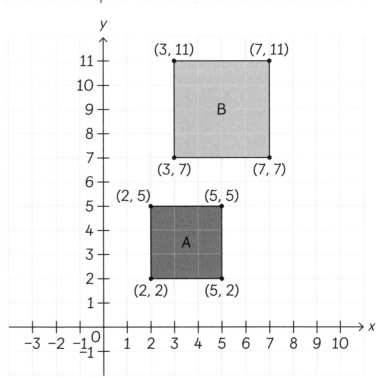

We can also use algebra to describe the coordinates.

If we describe the first coordinates of the first vertex as (x, y), we can describe the coordinates of the diagonally opposite vertex in terms of x and y.

Square A: coordinates of opposite vertices	
(2, 2) and (5, 5)	(5, 2) and (2, 5)
(x, y) and $(x + 3, y + 3)$	(s, t) and $(s - 3, t + 3)$

The x coordinate describes the distance from (0, 0) along the x axis.

The y coordinate describes the distance from (0, 0) along the y axis.

The vertex opposite (x, y) is 3 steps further along the x axis and 3 steps further along the y axis than (x, y).

Charles is correct.

How can the vertex diagonally opposite (c, d) be described?

Square B: coordinates of opposite vertices	
(3, 7) and (7, 11)	(7, 7) and (3, 11)
(a, b) and $(a + 4, b + 4)$	(c, d) and $(c - 4, d + 4)$

The vertex opposite (c, d) on square B is 4 steps back along the x axis and 4 steps further up the y axis than (c, d).

1 Complete the table.

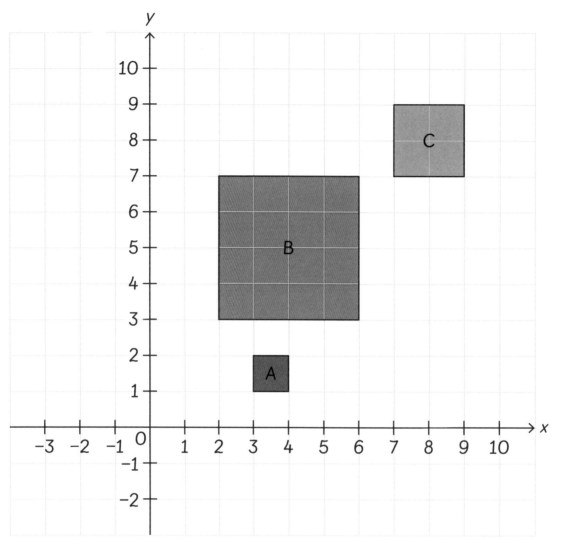

Square	Coordinates of opposite vertices	
A	(3, 1) and ([ ] , [ ])	(4, 1) and ([ ] , [ ])
B	(2, 3) and ([ ] , [ ])	(6, 3) and ([ ] , [ ])
C	(7, 7) and ([ ] , [ ])	(9, 7) and ([ ] , [ ])

2 (a) The coordinates for J are (x, y).
Find the coordinates for K, L and M.

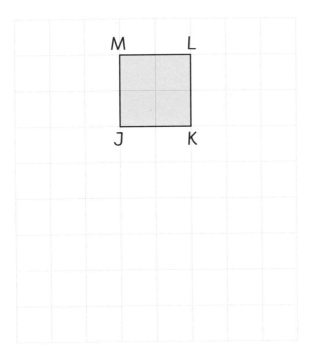

$K = (x + 2, y)$

$L = $ ⬚

$M = $ ⬚

(b) The coordinates for A are (x, y).
Find the coordinates for B, C and D.

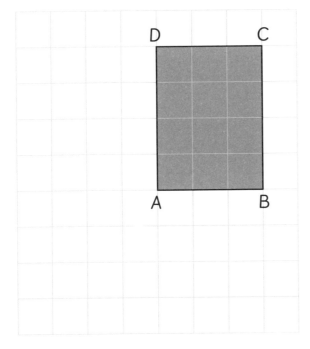

$B = (x + 3, y)$

$C = $ ⬚

$D = $ ⬚

Describing movement using algebra

Starter

Amira finds the coordinates of the new position of parallelogram ABCD after it has been reflected in the x axis.
She notices a pattern.
What do you think she notices?

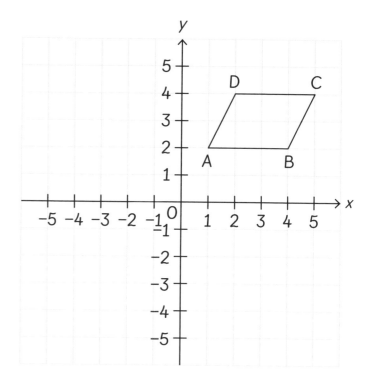

Example

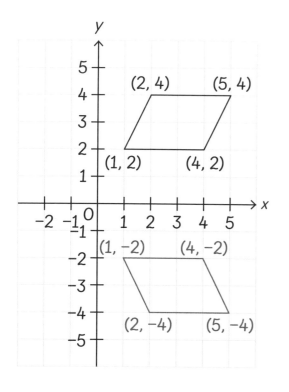

Point	Coordinates before reflection in the x axis	Coordinates after reflection in the x axis
A	(1, 2)	(1, −2)
B	(4, 2)	(4, −2)
C	(5, 4)	(5, −4)
D	(2, 4)	(2, −4)
	(x, y)	(x, −y)

We can express the reflection using algebra.

Practice

1 Parallelogram QRST is reflected in the *x* axis. Complete the table.

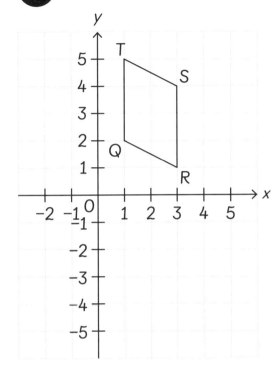

Point	Coordinates before reflection in the *x* axis	Coordinates after reflection in the *x* axis
Q	(,)	(,)
R	(,)	(,)
S	(,)	(,)
T	(,)	(,)
	(*x, y*)	(,)

2 Parallelogram ABCD is translated 2 units to the right and 4 units down. Complete the table.

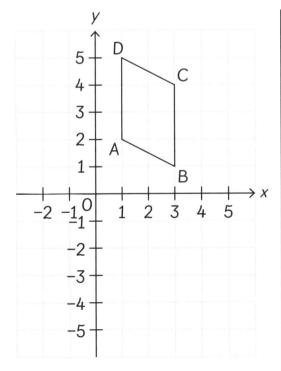

Point	Coordinates before translation	Coordinates after translation
A	(,)	(,)
B	(,)	(,)
C	(,)	(,)
D	(,)	(,)
	(*x, y*)	(,)

Prime numbers

Starter

Jacob has 6 stickers that he wants to stick on a page in his journal.
He notices he can arrange them into different rectangles.
How can he arrange the stickers in his journal?

Example

> Jacob can make 1 row of 6 stickers.

> He can make 2 rows of 3 stickers.

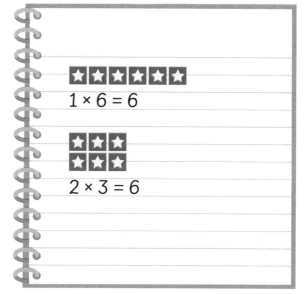

$1 \times 6 = 6$

$2 \times 3 = 6$

The factors of 6 are 1, 2, 3 and 6.

> What if Jacob has 7 stickers?

> I can only make a single rectangle.

$1 \times 7 = 7$

The factors of 7 are 1 and 7.

A prime number has only 2 factors, 1 and itself.

Numbers with more than 2 factors are called **composite numbers**. The number 6 is a composite number as it has 4 factors.

Prime numbers can only be made into a single rectangular arrangement.

Composite numbers can be made into multiple rectangular arrangements.

Practice

1 Find the factors of the following numbers and decide if they are prime or composite numbers.
Complete the table.

Number	Factors	Prime or composite
10		
25		
31		
43		
54		
53		

2 Make 3 different equations.
Use only prime numbers to fill in the blanks.

(a) ⬚ + ⬚ = 46

(b) ⬚ + ⬚ = 46

(c) ⬚ + ⬚ = 46

Four operations

Starter

Sam is at the fun fair.
He has a £10 note.
What is the maximum number
of balls he can buy?
How much change will he
receive?

Knock 'Em Down

Prices
9 🎾 for £2.70
5 🎾 for £1.85

Example

Sam can only buy balls in lots of 5 or 9.

9		$1 \times 2.70 = 2.70$
18		$2 \times 2.70 = 5.40$
27		$3 \times 2.70 = 8.10$

I know that £1.85 is close to £2.00. Sam can buy at least 5 lots of 5 balls.

25       $5 \times 1.85 = 9.25$

Is 25 the maximum number of balls Sam can buy or will buying a combination of lots of 9 and 5 give him more balls?

3 lots of 9 $3 \times 2.70 = 8.10$

1 lot of 5 $1 \times 1.85 = 1.85$

$8.10 + 1.85 = 9.95$

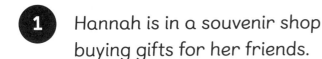
Sam can buy a maximum of 32 balls for £9.95.

10.00 − 9.95 = 0.05

Sam will receive 5p change.

Practice

1 Hannah is in a souvenir shop buying gifts for her friends.

Key rings
£1.40 each

Bookmarks
2 for £2.30

(a) What is the maximum amount of change Hannah could receive after buying 9 items?

The maximum amount of change Hannah could receive is £ ⬚.

(b) What is the minimum amount of change Hannah could receive after buying 9 items?

The minimum amount of change Hannah could receive is £ ⬚.

2 A restaurant buys 27 bags of potatoes to use in a vegetable curry. Each bag has a mass of 1.2 kg. The restaurant uses 670 g of potatoes for each pot of vegetable curry they make.
What is the mass of the remaining potatoes if the restaurant makes 29 pots of vegetable curry?

The mass of the remaining potatoes is ⬚ kg.

Multiplying fractions

Starter

Oak took $\frac{1}{8}$ of the remaining pizza.

What fraction of the whole pizza did Oak take?

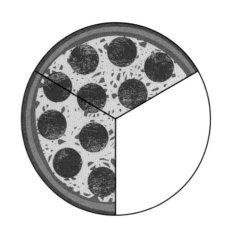

Example

Oak took $\frac{1}{8}$ of $\frac{2}{3}$ of a pizza.

$\frac{1}{12}$

As Oak took $\frac{1}{8}$, the remaining pizza must be 8 equal parts.

$$\frac{1}{8} \times \frac{2}{3} = \frac{1}{12}$$

Oak took $\frac{1}{12}$ of the whole pizza.

I found it this way.

$$\frac{1}{\underset{4}{8}} \times \frac{\overset{1}{2}}{3} = \frac{1}{12}$$

We can divide the numerator of one fraction and the denominator of the other fraction if they have a common factor.

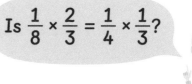

Is $\frac{1}{8} \times \frac{2}{3} = \frac{1}{4} \times \frac{1}{3}$?

$\frac{1}{8} \times \frac{2}{3} = \frac{1}{12}$

$\frac{1}{4} \times \frac{1}{3} = \frac{1}{12}$

$\frac{1}{8} \times \frac{2}{3} = \frac{1}{4} \times \frac{1}{3}$

Practice

Solve and give your answer in the simplest form.

1 Lulu's mum cut a cake into 10 equal pieces.
Lulu put 3 pieces on a plate for her and Elliott.

Elliott cut the pieces so he could take $\frac{3}{5}$ of the cake off the plate.

What fraction of the whole cake did Elliott take?

Elliott took ▢ of the whole cake.

2 A bag of rice was $\frac{7}{9}$ full. Emma took $\frac{1}{2}$ of the rice in the bag.

She used $\frac{6}{7}$ of the rice she took from the bag to cook a meal.

What fraction of the whole bag of rice did Emma use in her meal?

Emma used ▢ of the whole bag of rice in her meal.

Dividing fractions

Holly made 5 milkshakes for her friends.
She used an equal amount of chocolate syrup in each of the milkshakes.

If Holly used $\frac{2}{3}$ l of chocolate syrup altogether, what

fraction of a litre did she use in each milkshake?

Example

Divide each third into 5 equal parts.

$\frac{2}{3}$

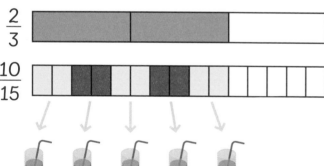

$\frac{10}{15}$

$\frac{2}{3} = \frac{10}{15}$

$\frac{2}{3} \div 5 = \frac{10}{15} \div 5$

$$= \frac{2}{15}$$

I know that $\frac{2}{3}$ divided by 5 is the same as finding $\frac{1}{5}$ of $\frac{2}{3}$.

$\frac{2}{3} \div 5 = \frac{1}{5} \times \frac{2}{3}$

$$= \frac{2}{15}$$

Holly used $\frac{2}{15}$ l of chocolate syrup in each milkshake.

Solve and give your answer in the simplest form.

1 Miss Fathima uses equal length pieces of string to tie name tags onto bags. She uses 8 pieces of string.

If Miss Fathima uses $\dfrac{6}{7}$ m of string altogether, what is the length of a single piece of string?

A single piece of string is ⬜ m long.

2 An equal amount of butter is given to each child in a cooking class.

The total mass of butter given to the children is $\dfrac{8}{9}$ kg.

If 12 children are given butter, what is the mass of butter each child gets?

Each child gets ⬜ kg of butter.

3 Ruby is making a tropical drink. She uses $\dfrac{1}{2}$ l of orange juice, $\dfrac{1}{4}$ l of pineapple juice and $\dfrac{1}{6}$ l of mango juice. She pours the tropical drink equally into 3 glasses.

What fraction of a litre of tropical drink does Ruby pour into each glass?

Ruby pours ⬜ l of tropical drink into each glass.

Multiplying decimals

Starter

Sam and 4 friends are going on a camping holiday. They each have a single person tent. The mass of each tent is 1.87 kg.

They put their tents into a large bag to bring on the train.

If the empty bag has a mass of 0.85 kg, what is the total mass of the bag and the tents?

Example

Start by finding the total mass of the tents.

$1.87 \times 5 = ?$

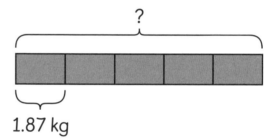

1.87 kg

Make sure each digit is in the right place.

$$
\begin{array}{r}
1 \ . \ 8 \ \ 7 \\
\times \qquad \ \ 5 \\
\hline
0 \ . \ 3 \ \ 5 \\
4 \ . \ 0 \\
+ \ 5 \\
\hline
9 \ . \ 3 \ \ 5 \\
\end{array}
$$

$\longrightarrow$ $0.07 \times 5 = 0.35$

$\longrightarrow$ $0.8 \ \times 5 = 4.0$

$\longrightarrow$ $1 \ \ \times 5 = 5$

$$
\begin{array}{r}
^4 1 \ . \ ^3 8 \ \ 7 \\
\times \qquad \ \ 5 \\
\hline
9 \ . \ 3 \ \ 5 \\
\end{array}
$$

I did it a different way.

$1.87 \times 5 = 9.35$

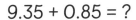

Add the mass of the bag to the total mass of the tents.

9.35 + 0.85 = ?

$$\begin{array}{r} {}^{1}9\ .\ {}^{1}3\ \ 5 \\ +\ \ \ \ 0\ .\ 8\ \ 5 \\ \hline 1\ \ 0\ .\ 2\ \ 0 \end{array}$$

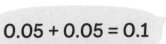

0.05 + 0.05 = 0.1

0.1 + 0.3 + 0.8 = 1.2

9.35 + 0.85 = 10.20
The total mass of the bag and tents is 10.2 kg.

Practice

1 A car wash uses 2.78 l of car washing liquid for every 100 l of water.
If the car wash used 800 l of water in one day, what was the total volume
of car washing liquid the car wash used?

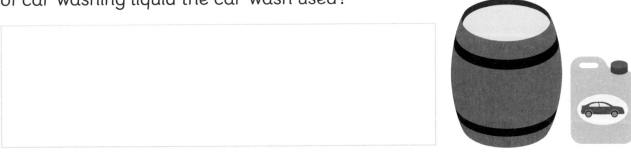

The total volume of car washing liquid the car wash used was ⬚ l.

2 A factory uses exactly 8.79 m of red thread in each multicoloured rug.
There are 100 m of red thread on each new spool.
If the factory started making multicoloured rugs using a new spool,
what was the length of red thread left on the spool after 7 rugs were made?

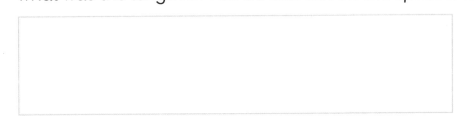

⬚ m of red thread was left on the spool after 7 rugs were made.

Dividing decimals

Starter

Charles and 6 friends each paid an equal amount towards a present for Oak.
The present cost £59.15.
How much did Charles and his friends each pay?

Example

Divide £59.15 by 7.

```
          8 . 4  5
  7 )  5  9 . 1  5
    -  5  6                    ⟶  7 × 8 = 56
          3 . 1  5
    -     2 . 8                ⟶  7 × 0.4 = 2.8
          0 . 3  5
    -     0 . 3  5             ⟶  7 × 0.05 = 0.35
                   0
```

```
        5915                        59.15
      ↙   ↓   ↘                  ↙    ↓    ↘
5600   280      35          56      2.8      0.35

5600 ÷ 7 = 800              56      ÷ 7 = 8
 280 ÷ 7 =  40             2.80 ÷ 7 = 0.4
  35 ÷ 7 =    5            0.35 ÷ 7 = 0.05
─────────────────         ─────────────────────
5915 ÷ 7 = 845            59.15 ÷ 7 = 8.45
```

I can also use my knowledge of multiples of 7 to help.

I know that 59.15 is 100 times smaller than 5915.

Charles and his friends each paid £8.45.

Practice

1 A gardener has a container holding 11.12 l of organic fertiliser. He uses all of the fertiliser on 4 rows of roses. He puts an equal amount of fertiliser on each of the 4 rows.
What is the volume of fertiliser that the gardener uses on a single row?

The gardener uses ☐ l of fertiliser on a single row.

2 Hannah's mum buys 12 sacks of pebbles to put on their driveway. In total, she buys 58.32 kg of pebbles.
If each sack of pebbles has an equal mass, what is the mass of a single sack?

The mass of a single sack of pebbles is ☐ kg.

Percentage

Starter

Ravi, Holly and Emma compared the prices of their skateboards. Ravi paid £48 for his skateboard. Holly paid 25% more than Ravi paid. Emma paid 30% less than Holly paid.
Who paid the least for their skateboard?

Example

We can start by saying the amount Ravi paid is 100%.

Find 25% to add to £48.

£48

Ravi | 25% | 25% | 25% | 25% |

£60

Holly | 25% | 25% | 25% | 25% | 25% |

£12

48 ÷ 4 = 12
48 + 12 = 60
Holly paid £60 for her skateboard.

We need to compare the amounts Holly and Emma paid for their skateboards.

Let the amount Holly paid be 100%.

£60

Holly | 10% | 10% | 10% | 10% | 10% | 10% | 10% | 10% | 10% | 10% |

£42

Emma | 10% | 10% | 10% | 10% | 10% | 10% | 10% |

Find 30% to take away from £60.

$60 \div 10 = 6$
$6 \times 3 = 18$
$60 - 18 = 42$

Emma paid £42 for her skateboard.
Emma paid the least for her skateboard.

Practice

1 Jacob had £240 of savings in the bank. He spent 25% of his savings on a new watch. After buying the watch, he spent 30% of his remaining savings on a jacket.
How much does Jacob now have saved in the bank?

Jacob now has £ ___ saved in the bank.

2 Ravi and Hannah had £90 between them. They shared the cost of a present for Charles. Ravi put 20% of his money towards the cost of the present and Hannah put 50% of her money towards the cost of the present. After buying the present, they had £63 left between them.

How much did Ravi have left? £ ___

How much did Hannah have left? £ ___

Ratio

Starter

The ratio of the number of pages in a novel to the number of pages in a comic book is 5 : 2. The ratio of the number of pages in the comic book to the number of pages in a booklet is 2 : 1.
If the total number of pages in the novel, comic book and booklet is 192, how many pages are in each book?

  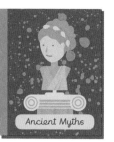

Example

We can use a bar model to represent the information we have.

Find the value of 1 unit.

192

8 units = 192
1 unit = 192 ÷ 8
       = 24

5 × 24 = 120
There are 120 pages in the novel.

2 × 24 = 48
There are 48 pages in the comic book.

1 × 24 = 24
There are 24 pages in the booklet.

1. In an orchard, the ratio of the number of apple trees to the number of pear trees is 5 : 3. There are 17 more cherry trees than pear trees in the orchard. If there are 248 trees in the orchard, how many cherry trees are there?

apple					

pear

cherry

248

17

There are ☐ cherry trees in the orchard.

2. The ratio of Ravi's savings to Emma's savings is 8 : 5.
The difference between the amount each of them has saved is £36.
How much has Ravi saved?

Ravi has saved £ ☐ .

3. Jacob painted a model train using blue, red and gold paint. The ratio of blue paint to red paint he used was 7 : 3. He used 25 ml less gold paint on the model train than red paint. In total, Jacob used 378 ml of paint.
Find the volume of paint he used for each colour.

blue paint ☐ ml   red paint ☐ ml   gold paint ☐ ml

Area

Starter

Lulu's father looks at a plan for garden allotments. He would like to rent allotment number 5 but wants to know its area first.

How can he find the area of allotment 5?

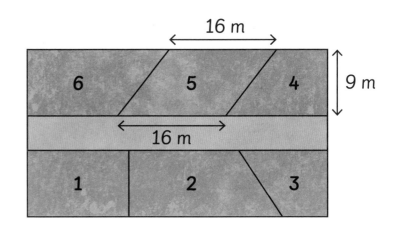

Example

Every parallelogram can be cut into 2 triangles that each have the same area.

We know the formula to find the area of a triangle.

The area of the parallelogram is twice the area of 1 triangle.

Area of a triangle = $\frac{1}{2} b \times h$

Area of a parallelogram = bh

$= 16 \times 9$

$= 144 \text{ m}^2$

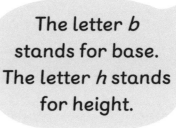

The letter b stands for base. The letter h stands for height.

$10 \times 16 = 160$

$9 \times 16 = 160 - 16$

The area of allotment 5 is 144 m².

Practice

1 Find the area of the parallelograms.

(a)

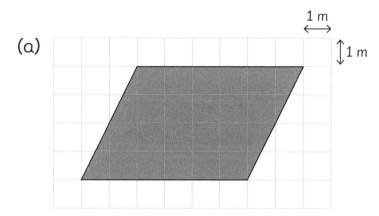

1 m

1 m

Area = [ ] m²

(b)

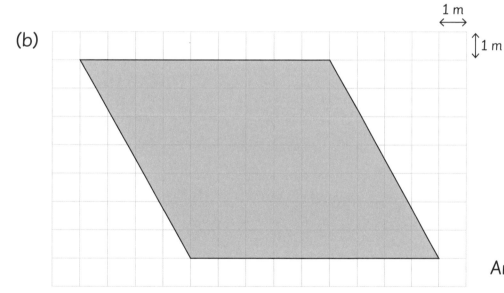

1 m

1 m

Area = [ ] m²

2 Use the measurements to find the area of the parallelogram.

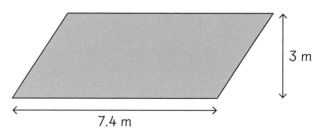

3 m

7.4 m

Area = [ ] m²

Angles

Starter

An octagon contains 5 identical squares. Can we find the sizes of ∠a and ∠b?

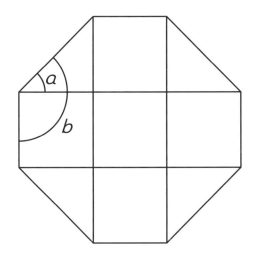

Example

We know the sides of the squares have equal lengths.

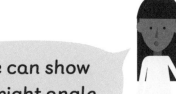
We can show the right angle.

As the triangle has 2 equal length sides, it will have 2 equal-sized angles.

We know that the internal angles in a triangle sum to 180°.

$$\angle a + \angle a + 90 = 180$$
$$\angle a + \angle a = 180 - 90$$
$$= 90$$

$$\angle a = \frac{90}{2}$$
$$= 45$$

$$\angle a = 45°$$

 We can now find ∠b.

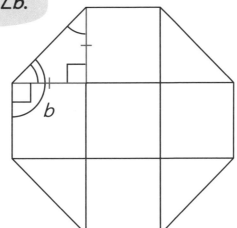

b

 We know ∠a = 45°.

∠a + 90 = ∠b

45 + 90 = 135

∠b = 135°

Practice

Find the sizes of the angles in the triangles.

1

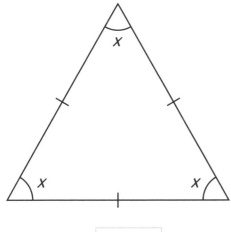

x

x   x

$x = $ [ ] °

2

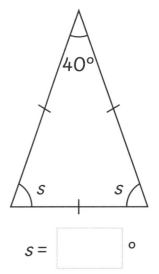

40°

s   s

$s = $ [ ] °

3

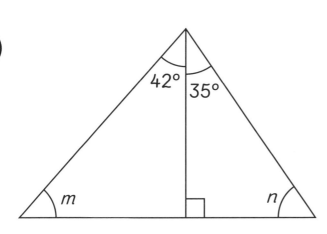

42° 35°

m   n

$m = $ [ ] °

$n = $ [ ] °

Reading graphs

Starter

Jacob and his family went on holiday around the world. When they returned to the UK, Jacob found 3 bus tickets in his rucksack. What was the cost of each bus ticket in British pounds (GBP)?

Example

We can use a line graph to convert the currencies.

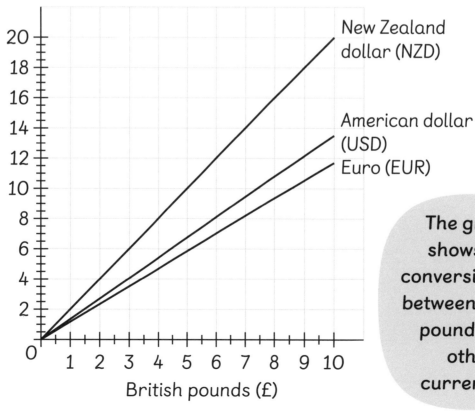

amount in each currency

British pounds (£)

New Zealand dollar (NZD)

American dollar (USD)

Euro (EUR)

The graph shows the conversion rate between British pounds and other currencies.

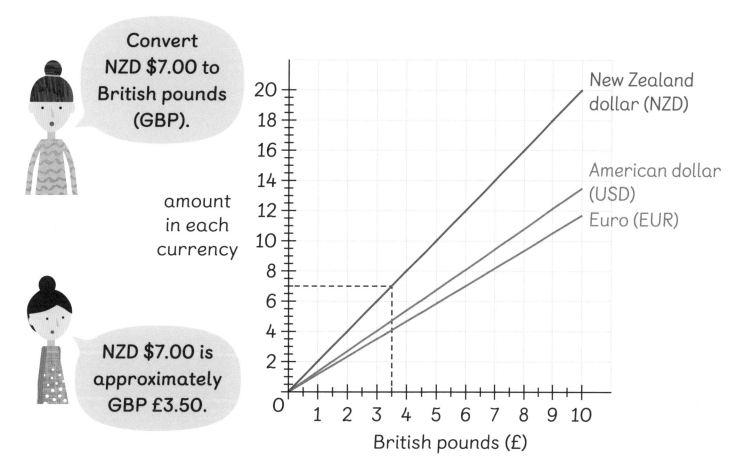

NZD $7.00 ≈ GBP £3.50

The cost of the bus ticket from New Zealand was approximately GBP £3.50.

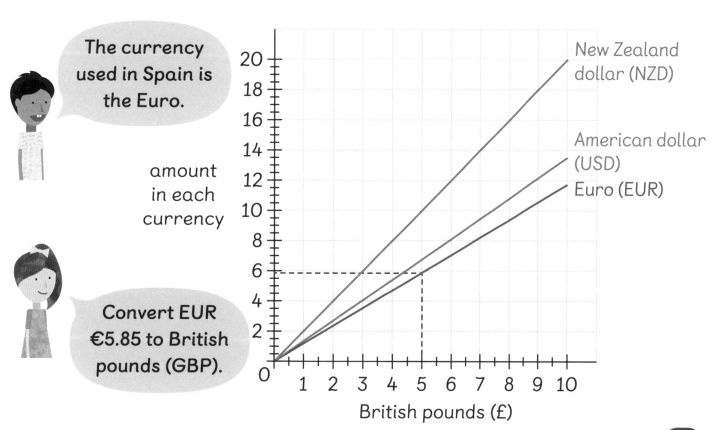

EUR €5.85 is approximately GBP £5.00.

EUR €5.85 ≈ GBP £5.00

The cost of the bus ticket from Spain was approximately GBP £5.00.

Convert USD $6.50 to British pounds (GBP).

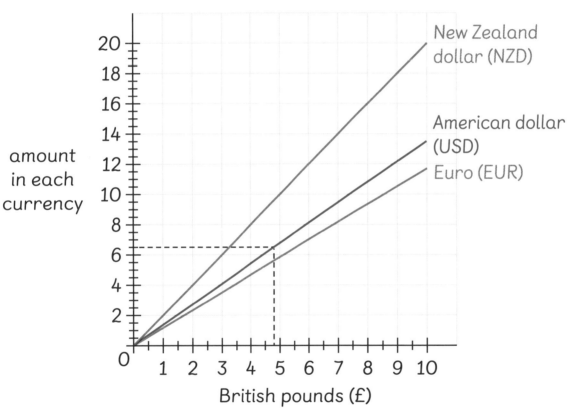

USD $6.50 is approximately GBP £4.80.

USD $6.50 ≈ GBP £4.80

The cost of the bus ticket from the USA was approximately GBP £4.80.

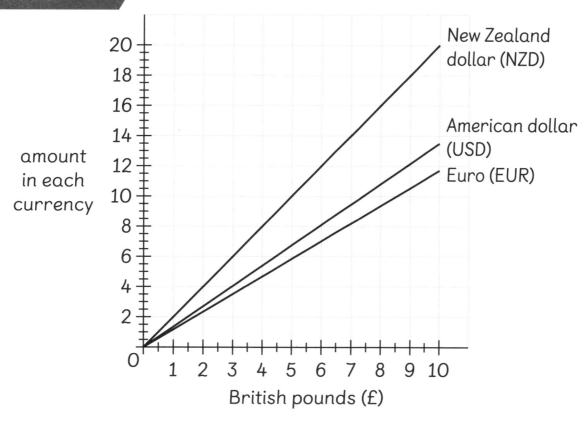

Jacob's mum received her bank statement which shows what she spent in each country in British pounds (GBP).

Find the cost of the items in their own currencies to complete the tables.

1

Items bought in New Zealand	Cost in GBP £	Approximate cost in NZD $
fish and chips	£7.50	
key ring	£5.80	

2

Items bought in Spain	Cost in GBP £	Approximate cost in EUR €
coffee and cake	£4.20	
bottle of water	£0.80	

3

Items bought in the USA	Cost in GBP £	Approximate cost in USD $
3 tacos	£3.70	
movie ticket	£6.95	

Averages

Starter

A factory packs mini fruit bars into bags. Each bag has to have a mean number of 35 mini fruit bars but can never have 3 more or 3 less than the mean number in a single bag. Random checks are made to ensure the bags have the correct number of mini fruit bars in them.

Bag 1	Bag 2	Bag 3	Bag 4	Bag 5	Bag 6
32	34	34	37	?	?

The difference between the number of mini fruit bars in bags 5 and 6 is 3. How many mini fruit bars do bags 5 and 6 contain?

Example

It is possible that there is more than one answer.

The 6 bags must contain 210 mini fruit bars in total to have a mean number of 35 in each bag.

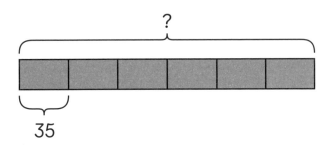

$6 \times 35 = 210$

If we know the 6 bags must contain 210 mini fruit bars and the total number in 4 bags, we can find the difference.

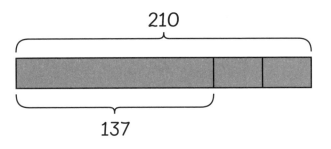

$210 - 137 = 73$

Bags 5 and 6 must have a total of 73 mini fruit bars.

Bag 5	Bag 6	Total	Difference
38	35	73	3
37	36	73	1
36	37	73	1
35	38	73	3

When bag 5 contains 38 mini fruit bars, bag 6 must contain 35 mini fruit bars.
When bag 5 contains 35 mini fruit bars, bag 6 must contain 38 mini fruit bars.

Practice

1 On a farm there are 8 paddocks with a mean number of 37 sheep in each paddock. There are 222 sheep in total in the first 6 paddocks. There are 12 fewer sheep in the seventh paddock than there are in the eighth paddock. How many sheep are in the seventh and eighth paddocks?

There are ⬚ sheep in the seventh paddock.

There are ⬚ sheep in the eighth paddock.

2 Holly wants a total score of 185 points once she has played 10 games. In her first 8 games, she gets a mean score of 17.5 points per game. How many points in total does Holly need to get in her final 2 games to have a total score of 185 points?

Holly needs to get ⬚ points in her final 2 games to have a total score of 185 points.

Answers

Page 5

Pattern number	Number of pink squares	Number of green squares
1	1	2
2	2	3
3	3	4
4	4	5
5	5	6
10	10	11
a	a	$a+1$

Page 7

1

Input	7	9	13	35	81
Output	12	14	18	40	86

2

Input	3	5	10	12	300
Output	9	15	30	36	900

3   input   output   input   output   input   output

(b) $4 \rightarrow 12$ $6 \rightarrow 18$ $w \rightarrow 3w$

(c) $9 \rightarrow 18$ $12 \rightarrow 21$ $s \rightarrow s+9$

Page 9   **1**   input   output   input   output   input   output

(a) $10 \rightarrow 5$ $16 \rightarrow 8$ $a \rightarrow \dfrac{a}{2}$

(b) $5 \rightarrow 20$ $7 \rightarrow 28$ $a \rightarrow 4a$

2

Pattern number	Number of toothpicks
n	$2n+1$
1	$2 \times 1 + 1 = 3$
2	$2 \times 2 + 1 = 5$
5	$2 \times 5 + 1 = 11$

Page 11   **1 (a)** C = 3 × 3.20 – 0.40 = 9.60 – 0.40 = 9.20. The total cost of 3 cheese toasties is £9.20.
(b) m = 2.70; C = 3 × 2.70 = 8.10 – 0.40 = 7.70. The cost of 3 hot dogs is £7.70.   **2 (a)** P = 4   **(b)** P = 4.75

Page 13   **1 (a)** y = 15   **(b)** y = 18   **2 (a)** s = 14   **(b)** s = 9   **(c)** s = 12   **(d)** s = 8   **(e)** s = 5

Page 16   **1**

Square	Coordinates of opposite vertices	
A	(3, 1) and (4, 2)	(4, 1) and (3, 2)
B	(2, 3) and (6, 7)	(6, 3) and (2, 7)
C	(7, 7) and (9, 9)	(9, 7) and (7, 9)

Page 17   **2 (a)** L = $(x + 2, y + 2)$, M = $(x, y + 2)$ **(b)** C = $(x + 3, y + 4)$, D = $(x, y + 4)$

Page 19 1

Point	Coordinates before reflection in the x axis	Coordinates after reflection in the x axis
Q	(1, 2)	(1, −2)
R	(3, 1)	(3, −1)
S	(3, 4)	(3, −4)
T	(1, 5)	(1, −5)
	(x, y)	(x, −y)

2

Point	Coordinates before translation	Coordinates after translation
A	(1, 2)	(3, −2)
B	(3, 1)	(5, −3)
C	(3, 4)	(5, 0)
D	(1, 5)	(3, 1)
	(x, y)	(x + 2, y − 4)

Page 21 1

Number	Factors	Prime or composite
10	1, 2, 5, 10	composite
25	1, 5, 25	composite
31	1, 31	prime
43	1, 43	prime
54	1, 2, 3, 6, 9, 18, 27, 54	composite
53	1, 53	prime

2 Answers will vary. For example: 23 + 23 = 46, 43 + 3 = 46, 29 + 17 = 46

Page 23 1 (a) The maximum amount of change Hannah could receive is £9.40. **(b)** The minimum amount of change Hannah could receive is £7.40. **2** The mass of the remaining potatoes is 12.97 kg.

Page 25 1 Elliott took $\frac{9}{50}$ of the whole cake. **2** Emma used $\frac{1}{3}$ of the whole bag of rice in her meal.

Page 27 1 $\frac{6}{7} \div 8 = \frac{1}{8} \times \frac{6}{7} = \frac{6}{56} = \frac{3}{28}$. A single piece of string is $\frac{3}{28}$ m long. **2** $\frac{8}{9} \div 12 = \frac{1}{12} \times \frac{8}{9} = \frac{8}{108} = \frac{2}{27}$. Each child gets $\frac{2}{27}$ kg of butter. **3** $\frac{1}{2} + \frac{1}{4} + \frac{1}{6} = \frac{3}{4} + \frac{1}{6} = \frac{9}{12} + \frac{2}{12} = \frac{11}{12}$; $\frac{11}{12} \div 3 = \frac{1}{3} \times \frac{11}{12} = \frac{11}{36}$. Ruby pours $\frac{11}{36}$ l of tropical drink into each glass.

Page 29 1 The total volume of car washing liquid the car wash used was 22.24 l. **2** 38.47 m of red thread was left on the spool after 7 rugs were made.

Page 31 1 The gardener uses 2.78 l of fertiliser on a single row. **2** The mass of a single sack of pebbles is 4.86 kg.

Page 33 1 Jacob now has £126 saved in the bank.

2 Cost of the present

Money left

£27 The bars show the amounts that each of them spent and £63 what they had left. $\frac{2}{10}$ (20%) of Ravi's savings and half (50%) £36 of Hannah's savings is £27.

To find the difference between what they spent on the present and what they had left, we can subtract the part of the bar that is the same, leaving Ravi's $\frac{6}{10}$. 63 − 27 = 36. So, we know that $\frac{6}{10}$ is equal to 36. If $\frac{6}{10}$ is £36, then $\frac{1}{10}$ is equal to £6.

Ravi started with £60. Hannah started with £30. Ravi put £12 and Hannah put £15 towards the cost of the present. After buying the present, Ravi has £48 left. Hannah has £15 left.

Page 35 1 248 − 17 = 231, 231 ÷ 11 = 21, 1 unit = 21. 21 × 5 = 105 (apple trees), 21 × 3 = 63 (pear trees), 63 + 17 = 80. There are 80 cherry trees in the orchard. **2** 8 − 5 = 3, 36 ÷ 3 = 12, 1 unit = 12. 12 × 8 = 96. Ravi has saved £96. **3** 378 + 25 = 403, 403 ÷ 13 = 31, 1 unit = 31. 31 × 7 = 217 (blue), 31 × 3 = 93 (red), 93 − 25 = 68 (gold). blue paint − 217 ml, red paint − 93 ml, gold paint − 68 ml

Page 37 1 (a) Area = 24 m² **(b)** Area = 63 m² **2** Area = 22.2 m²

Page 39 1 x = 60° **2** s = 70° **3** m = 48°, n = 55°

Answers continued

Page 43 **1**

Items bought in New Zealand	Cost in GBP £	Approximate cost in NZD $
fish and chips	£7.50	$15.00
key ring	£5.80	$11.60

2

Items bought in Spain	Cost in GBP £	Approximate cost in EUR €
coffee and cake	£4.20	€4.90
bottle of water	£0.80	€0.90

3

Items bought in the USA	Cost in GBP £	Approximate cost in USD $
3 tacos	£3.70	$5.00
movie ticket	£6.95	$9.40

Page 45 **1** There are 31 sheep in the seventh paddock. There are 43 sheep in the eighth paddock.

2 Holly needs to get 45 points in her final 2 games to have a total score of 185 points.